The Greatest
LOVE SONGS
Of The 21st Century

Published by

Wise Publications
14-15 Berners Street, London W1T 3LJ, UK.

Exclusive Distributors:

Music Sales Limited
Distribution Centre, Newmarket Road,
Bury St Edmunds, Suffolk IP33 3YB, UK.

Music Sales Pty Limited
120 Rothschild Avenue, Rosebery,
NSW 2018, Australia.

Order No. AM986832
ISBN 1-84609-711-8
This book © Copyright 2006 Wise Publications,
a division of Music Sales Limited.

Front cover photo courtesy of Jupiter Images.
Back cover photos courtesy of LFI.

Printed in the EU.

www.musicsales.com

The Greatest
LOVE SONGS
Of The 21st Century

Wise Publications
part of The Music Sales Group

London/New York/Paris/Sydney/Copenhagen/Berlin/Madrid/Tokyo

Your Guarantee of Quality

As publishers, we strive to produce every book
to the highest commercial standards.

The book has been carefully designed
to minimise awkward page turns and to
make playing from it a real pleasure.

Particular care has been given to specifying
acid-free, neutral-sized paper made from pulps
which have not been elemental chlorine bleached.

This pulp is from farmed sustainable forests and
was produced with special regard for the environment.

Throughout, the printing and binding have been
planned to ensure a sturdy, attractive publication
which should give years of enjoyment.

If your copy fails to meet our high standards,
please inform us and we will gladly replace it.

The Closest Thing To Crazy

Words & Music by Mike Batt

1. How can I think I'm stand-ing strong yet
2. How can you make me fall a-part then

feel the air be-neath my feet?
break my fall with lov-ing lies?

How can I___ have got in so deep?
How can a - ny - one feel so wild?

Why did I___ fall in love with you?
How can a - ny - one feel so blue?
This is the

clos - est thing___ to cra - zy I have ev - er been.___ Feel - ing

twen - ty two,___ act - ing sev - en - teen.___ This is the

near-est thing_ to cra-zy I have ev - er known._ I was

nev - er cra - zy on my own___ and

now I know_ that there's a link be-tween_ the two.__

Be - ing close_ to cra - zi - ness_ and

9

Come What May

Words & Music by David Baerwald

Rather slow

Nev - er knew I could feel____ like this,____ like I've____ nev - er seen____ the sky____

____ be - fore. Want to van - ish in - side____ your kiss,____

ev - 'ry day____ I love____ you more and____ more. Lis - ten to____ my heart____ can you

Don't Know Why

Words & Music by Jesse Harris

Verse 3:
Out across the endless sea
I will die in ecstasy
But I'll be a bag of bones
Driving down the road alone.

My heart is drenched in wine etc.

Verse 4:
Something has to make you run
I don't know why I didn't come
I feel as empty as a drum
I don't know why I didn't come
I don't know why I didn't come
I don't know why I didn't come

19

Dry Your Eyes

Words & Music by Mike Skinner

1. In one single moment your whole life can turn 'round. I stand there for a minute staring straight into the ground,
(Verses 2 & 3 see block lyrics)

looking to the left slightly then looking back down. World feels like it's caved in, proper sorry frown.

A

Please let me show you where we could only just be for us. I can change and I can grow or we could adjust.

A/D

The wicked thing about us is we always have trust, we can even have an open relationship if you must.

A

I look at her, she stares almost straight back at me, but her eyes glaze over like she's looking straight through me

D

Then her eyes must have closed for what seems an eternity. When they open up she's looking down at her feet.

21

Verse 2:
So then I moved my hand up from down by my side
Shaking, my life was crashing before my eyes
Turned the palm of my hand up to face the skies
Touched the bottom of her chin and let out a sigh
'Cause I can't imagine my life without you and me
There's things I can't imagine doing and things I can't imagine seeing
It weren't supposed to be easy surely?
Please, please I'm begging, please
She brings her hands up towards where my hands rested
She wraps her fingers 'round mine with the softness she's blessed with
She peels away my fingers, looks at me and then gestures
By pushing my hand away to my chest from hers.

Verse 3:
Trying to pull her close out of bare desperation
Put my arms around her, trying to change what she's saying
Pull my head level with hers so she might engage in
Look into her eyes to make her listen again.
I'm not gonna fuckin', just fuckin' leave it all now
'Cause you said it would be forever and that was your vow
And you're gonna let our thing simply crash and fall down
You're well out of order now, this is well out of town.
She pulls away my arms are tightly clamped around her waist
Gently pushes me back as she looks at me straight
Turns around so she's now got her back to my face
Takes one step forward, looks back and then walks away.

25

Eternity

Words & Music by Robbie Williams & Guy Chambers

1. Close your eyes so you don't feel them,
2. Yes - ter - day when you were walk - ing,

they don't need to see you cry.
we talked a - bout your Ma and Dad;

I can't pro - mise I will
what they did that made you

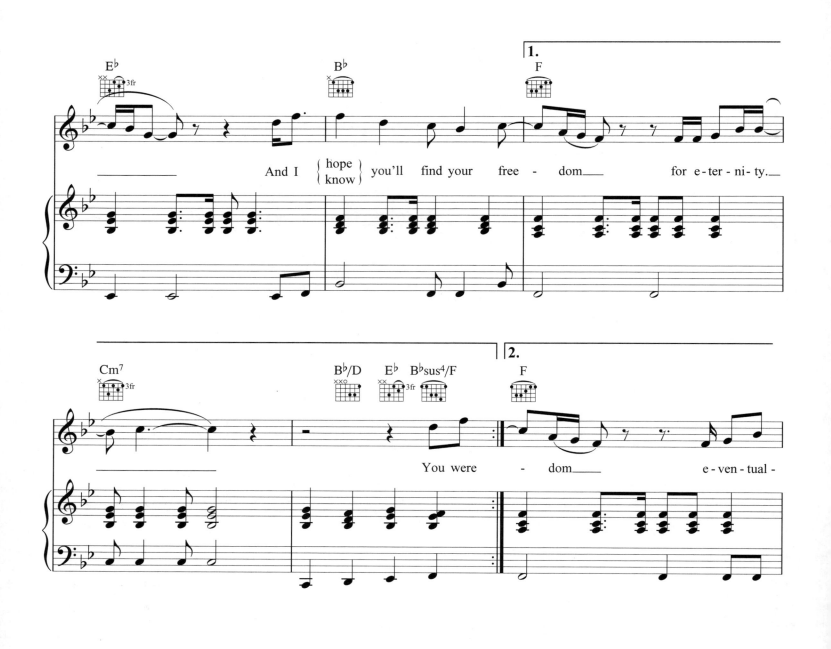

And I {hope / know} you'll find your free - dom___ for e - ter - ni - ty.___

You were - dom___ e - ven - tual -

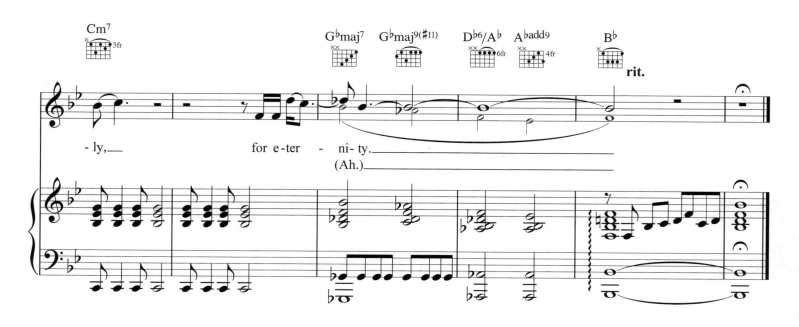

- ly,___ for e - ter - ni - ty.___

(Ah.)___

Fool Again

Words & Music by Jorgen Elofsson,
Per Magnusson & David Kreuger

33

Verse 2:
Baby, you should've called me
When you were lonely
When you needed me to be there
Sadly, you never gave me
Too many chances
To show you how much I care.

I should've seen it coming *etc.*

Hero

Words & Music by Enrique Iglesias,
Paul Barry & Mark Taylor

Oh._____ I just wan - na hold   you.___

Verse 2:
Would you swear that you'll always be mine?
Would you lie? Would you run and hide?
Am I in too deep? Have I lost my mind?
I don't care, you're here tonight.

I can be your hero baby *etc.*

If Tomorrow Never Comes

Words & Music by Garth Brooks & Kent Blazy

Verse 2:
'Cause I've lost loved ones in my life
Who never knew how much I loved them
Now I live with the regret
The natural feelings for them never were revealed
So I made a promise to myself
To say each day how much she means to me
And avoid that circumstance
Where there's no second chance
To tell her how I feel.

If tomorrow never comes *etc.*

If You're Not The One

Words & Music By Daniel Bedingfield

side.   I don't wan-na run a-way_ but I___ can't take it, I___ don't un-der-stand._

___ If I'm not made_ for you_ then why_ does my heart tell_ me that I am?_

___ Is there a-ny way_ that I___ can stay___ in your arms?_

Repeat to fade

Drums

51

Leave Right Now

Words & Music by Francis White

- gain.

Mm,_____   mm,__ mm, mm.__

Think I'd bet-ter leave right now   be-fore I fall an-y deep-er,

I think I'd bet-ter leave____ right____ now_____   I'm feel-ing weak-er and weak-er,

some-bo-dy bet-ter show me__ how_____   be-fore I fall an-y deep-er,__

If You Come Back

Words & Music by Ray Ruffin, Nicole Formescu,
Ian Hope & Lee Brennan

59

Verse 2:
I watched you go
Taking my heart with you
Oh, yes you did
Every time I try to reach you on the phone
Baby, you're never there
Girl, you're never home.

So if I did something wrong *etc.*

Like A Star

Words & Music by Corinne Bailey Rae

Lost Without You

Words & Music by Bridget Benenate & Matthew Gerrard

1. I know I can be a lit-tle stub-born some-times and I'd say
2. How'm I ev-er gon-na get rid of these blues?

ba - by since__ you've gone__ I ad - mit that I___ was wrong.____
On - ly you__ could make it right, no, I'm not too proud to say,_____

All I know is I'm lost__ with - out__ you, I'm not gon - na lie.__

How'm I gon - na be strong with - out__ you, I need you by__ my side._

If we ev - er said we'd nev - er be to - geth - er and we end - ed with good-bye,__ don't know

Never Had A Dream Come True

Words & Music by Cathy Dennis & Simon Ellis

74

al-ways be my ba-by. I nev-er found the words to say you're the one I think a - bout each day. And I know no

mat - ter where life takes me to, a part of me will al - ways be

with you, yeah. You'll al-ways be the dream that fills my

head. Yes you will, say you will. You know you will, oh, ba-by. You'll al-ways be the one I know I'll

Verse 2:
Somewhere in my memory
I've lost all sense of time
And tomorrow can never be
'Cause yesterday is all that fills my mind
There's no use looking back or wondering
How it should be now or might have been
All this I know but still
I can't find ways to let you go.

I never had a dream come true *etc.*

Stop!

Words & Music by Samantha Brown,
Gregg Sutton & Bruce Brody

1. All that I have is all that you've giv-en me,
(2.) walk a-way,

did you nev-er wor-ry that I'd come to de-pend on you?
but it's not that ea-sy when your soul is torn in two.

Songbird

Words & Music by Christine McVie

2. To_____ you_____

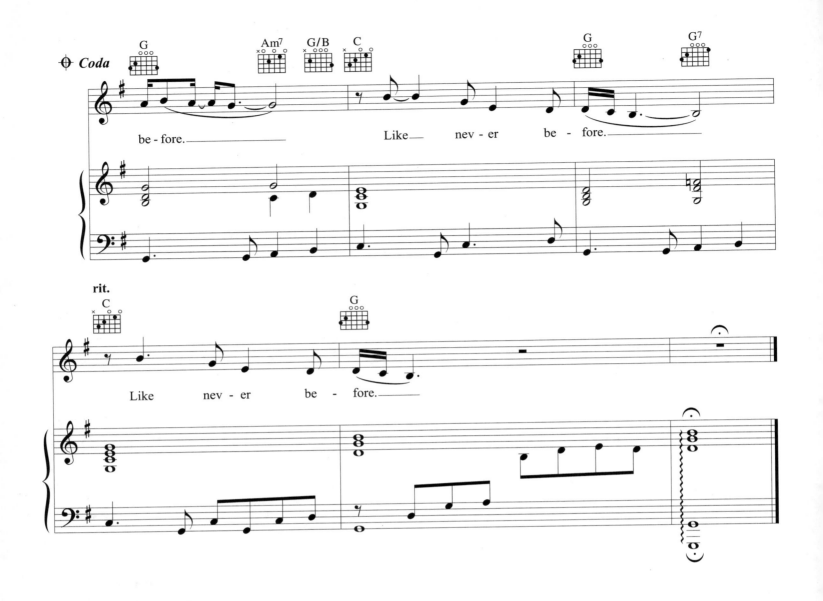

Verse 2:
To you I would give the world
To you I'd never be cold
'Cause I feel that when I'm with you
It's alright
I know it's right.

And the songbirds keep singing *etc.*

This Love

Words & Music by Adam Levine, James Valentine,
Jesse Carmichael, Mickey Madden & Ryan Dusick

1. I was___ so high___ I did___ not re-cog-nise___ the fire___ burn - ing
2. I tried___ my best to feed___ her ap - pe - tite,___ to keep her com - ing

many times be - fore.

And her heart is

break - ing in front____ of me____ and I have no choice 'cause

I won't say good-bye an - y - more.____

Whoa,____

whoa,____

whoa.____

This Year's Love

Words & Music by David Gray

1. This year's love had bet-ter last;_____ hea-ven knows, it's high
(Verse 2 see block lyric)

time.___ I've been wait-ing on my own too___ long.___

And when you hold me like you do___ it feels___ so___ right,___ oh now,___

I start to for - get how my heart gets torn when that
(Verse 3 see block lyric)

hurt gets thrown; feel-ing___ like I can't___ go on.___

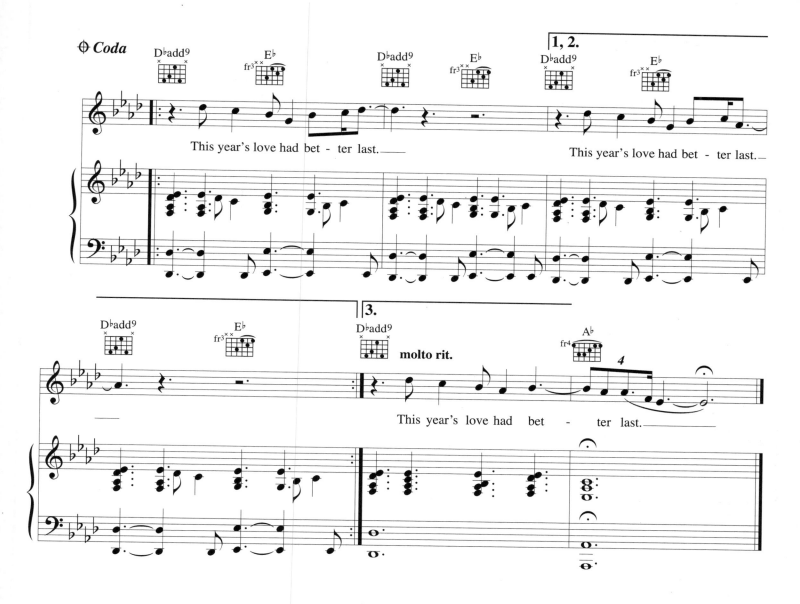

Verse 2:

Turning circles and time again
It cuts like a knife, oh now
If you love me I got to know for sure
'Cause it takes something more this time
Than sweet, sweet lies, oh now
Before I open up my arms and fall
Losing all control
Every dream inside my soul
When you kiss me on that midnight street
Sweep me off my feet
Singing ain't this life so sweet.

Verse 3:

'Cause who's to worry if our hearts get torn
When that hurt gets thrown?
Don't you know this life goes on?
Won't you kiss me on that midnight street
Sweep me off my feet
Singing ain't this life so sweet?

A Thousand Miles

Words & Music by Vanessa Carlton

1,3. Mak-ing my way down town, walk-ing fast;
(Verse 2 see block lyric)

— fac-es pass,— and I'm home-bound.

to the sky, do you think time would pass me by? 'Cause

you know I'd walk a thou-sand miles if I could just see you

to-night.

2. It's

98

99

Verse 2:
It's always times like these
When I think of you
And I wonder if you ever think of me.
'Cause everything's so wrong
And I don't belong
Living in your precious memory.
'Cause I need you
And I miss you
And now I wonder:

If I could fall into the sky *etc.*

Trouble With Love Is

Words & Music by Evan Rogers,
Carl Sturken & Kelly Clarkson

1. Love can be a ma-ny splen-doured thing, can't de-ny the joy it brings:
2. Now I was once a fool, it's true, I played the game by all the rules;

tear you up in - side,_____ make your heart be - lieve a___ lie._____ It's

strong - er than your pride._____ The trou - ble with love_ is_____ it does - n't

care how fast you fall,_____ and you can't re - fuse_ the call._____ See, you've

1. got no say at all,_____ oh._____

2. got no say at all._____

Ev-'ry-time I turn a-round,_____ I think I've_ got it all_ fig-ured out.

My heart keeps call-ing, and I keep on fall-ing ov-er and ov-er a-gain._____

This sad sto-ry al-ways ends_ the_ same:_____ me_ stand-ing in the pour-ing rain._

D.S. *repeat chorus to fade*

It seems,_ no mat-ter what I do,_____ it tears_ my heart in two._____ The trou-ble with

Unfaithful

Words & Music by Mikkel Eriksen,
Tor Erik Hermansen & Shaffer Smith

be the rea - son why.___ Ev-'ry-time I walk out the door I see him die a

lit - tle more___ in - side.___ I don't wan-na hurt him an - y - more

I don't wan-na take a - way___ his life.___ I don't wan - na be___

a mur-der-er.___

Yellow

Words & Music by Guy Berryman, Jon Buckland,
Will Champion & Chris Martin

Guitar Tuned:

① = D♯   ④ = B
② = B   ⑤ = A
③ = G   ⑥ = E

And it was called— yel - low.— So then I took my—

— turn, oh, what a thing to've— done.—

And it was all— yel - low.—

Your skin,— oh yeah, your skin and bones— turn— in - -

114

Verse 2:
I swam across, I jumped across for you.
Oh, what a thing to do.
'Cause you were all yellow,
I drew a line, I drew a line for you,
Oh, what a thing to do,
And it was all yellow.

Your skin, oh yeah, your skin and bones
Turn into something beautiful,
And you know, for you I'd bleed myself dry,
For you I'd bleed myself dry.

You're Beautiful

Words & Music by Sacha Skarbek,
James Blunt & Amanda Ghost

My life is bril - liant.

You Give Me Something

Words & Music by Francis White & James Morrison

late._____ And the words_____ that I_____ could nev- er say_

gon-na come out an- y- way,_____ oh.

'Cause you_____ give_ me_____ some-

-thing_____ that makes me scared al - right.___ This could_ be_____ no-

127

123456789